THE FACES OF GRIEF

Marian Talley-Cunningham

A WOMEN'S BIBLE STUDY

*To Camille with Love —
God Bless!*

Jean

journeyforth®

Greenville, South Carolina

The Faces of Grief

Marian Talley-Cunningham

Cover design by Rita Golden
Page layout by Kelley Moore

© 2007 by BJU Press
Greenville, South Carolina 29614
JourneyForth Books is a division of BJU Press

Printed in the United States of America
All rights reserved

ISBN 978-1-59166-757-5

15   14   13   12   11   10   9   8   7   6   5   4   3   2

CONTENTS

ACKNOWLEDGMENTS

This book is dedicated to those who have just started their journey of grief, those who have been on their journey for a while, and others who would like to help those who are traveling this road of grief. Many who are grieving do not understand their grief, and those who have not had a significant loss often do not understand or know how to help those who have experienced a loss.

I would also like to thank my family who has supported me in my journey, to my daughter, Louise Collins, who was helpful with her editing skills, and to my good friend Brenda Dooley, who used the rough draft of the book when she suddenly lost her husband. Her insight and suggestions in many areas were of great value.

Also a special dedication to my widow and widower friends who have walked beside me with words of encouragement and who have allowed me to walk beside them in their time of loss.

May the Lord use this book to help and encourage you as you seek the uncharted path before you. You will survive.

Psalm 138:8

WHY GOD? WHY NOW?
WHY IN THIS WAY?

*M*any have spent sleepless night asking the following questions: Why did God allow the death of my loved one; why at this time in my life; why did the death come so suddenly; why did he have to suffer so long? The "whys" we often ask are normal. They are part of the grieving and healing process. If the death of your loved one was preceded by a lengthy illness, your "whys" may have started at the time of diagnosis or at the time of the accident. If the loss was sudden, your "whys" have been there day and night from the time of death. What are some of the "whys" you have asked?

1. In John 11:21–26 who asked the "why" questions?

_____

Martha had a questioning spirit. She knew she would see Lazarus in heaven, but that did not satisfy her. She needed to feel the physical presence of her brother and knew her Lord had the power to bring him back to life. You can take great comfort in verses 25–26, knowing your loved one is in heaven, but it is the physical presence of your loved one that you miss.

2. What time of day do you miss your loved one the most? What are some activities that you miss?

_____

_____

_____

_____

3. You have a promise in Hebrews 13:5. Who has promised to be close to you and never leave? How can you claim this promise now, even in the midst of your loss?

_____

_____

_____

_____

You may doubt the goodness of the Lord in difficult times. You may wonder if He has your best interest at heart. Remember that everything that comes into your life is first filtered through the hands of an all-knowing God. Psalm 37:23 reminds us, "The steps of a good man are ordered by the Lord."

4. How can Psalm 37:23 be a source of encouragement in times of doubt?

_____

_____

_____

Once when the disciples were on the sea with our Lord, a storm came that threatened to destroy the boat and drown the men. Read the account of this event in Matthew 8:23–26. The men who had followed our Lord and watched Him perform miracles were suddenly doubtful that He could calm the sea.

5. What are some of the "great storms" you are facing right now?

_____

_____

_____

_____

6. Waiting can be hard when you have so many unanswered questions. Read Isaiah 41:10 for encouragement. What does this verse promise?

_____

_____

7. Fear is a real part of grief, but the God Who gave the promise in Isaiah 41:10 is also the God Who can sustain and give you peace in the midst of your storm. What can you claim as an assurance or promise of your own from the following verses?

Job 23:10_____

_____

_____

_____

Psalm 50:15_____

_____

_____

_____

Psalm 56:3_____

_____

_____

_____

Jeremiah 29:11_____

_____

_____

_____

II Corinthians 4:8–9_____

_____

_____

_____

8. Before the illness and death of your loved one, maybe your life was running smoothly. You had plans for the future and goals you wanted to reach. Death has put a "crooked path" before you. Read Ecclesiastes 7:13. What would you consider to be some "crooked paths" right now?

_____

_____

_____

_____

Trust God even if the path is crooked. Trust Him if you do not understand the events and circumstances. In order to trust God, you must view your adverse circumstances through the eyes of faith. This is difficult. Trusting God in adversity comes through the Word of God alone.

9. Jeremiah wrote the book of Lamentations when he was experiencing great distress in his life. Lamentations 3:37–38 tells us that God allows evil times and good times. The word *evil* may be translated "calamities." Death is viewed as a calamity, but think for a moment about the good times of the past. Recall below some of the good memories you shared with your loved one. Keep this list handy

and add to it as you recall more of those times. Think on these good times in lonely and discouraging days.

_____

_____

_____

_____

_____

10. Have you considered the care that God has for the sparrow? Read Matthew 10:29–31. The sparrow is a creature that is small and common, yet it is mentioned in this passage. In contrast to the sparrow, where do you see yourself in God's care? Read the following verses and write out in your own words what they mean to you in your grief.

Psalm 91:1–2_____

_____

_____

Proverbs 16:9_____

_____

_____

Isaiah 40:31_____

_____

_____

11. You have found some verses that give you encouragement and assurance, but still the question of "why" may be in your mind. What does Job 5:7 say about pain and suffering?

_____

_____

12. Let us consider others in the Bible who faced the death of someone they loved. Read the following verses and identify who died and who was left to mourn.

	Who died?	Who was left to mourn?
Genesis 23:2	_____	_____
	_____	_____
Genesis 24:67	_____	_____
	_____	_____
Luke 7:12–13	_____	_____
	_____	_____
John 19:30; 20:11	_____	_____
	_____	_____

Death is never easy. Mourning is natural. It is an intruder into our orderly world. You have loved; therefore, you will hurt.

13. Someone may have quoted Romans 8:28 to you. It reads, "And we know that all things work together for good to them that love God, to them who are the called according to his purpose." This verse can be a comforting verse, and yet it is often doubted and misunderstood. Have you found this verse to be comforting in the midst of your loss? Explain.

_____

_____

_____

_____

Can you find comfort in this verse? You will find comfort only when you see God in the middle of your trial. Does God really know what He is doing? That may take a long time to realize. Have you doubted this verse? Do you have a hard time understanding the circumstances that this verse implies?

14. The first three words of Romans 8:28 are "And we know." It is often hard to say you *know* something when you are in the midst of trials and testing. It is often hard to say you *know* when you *feel* so alone and untrusting. Look at the following verses and write out how they can be a comfort to you.

   Romans 5:3–4_____

   _____

   _____

   _____

   James 1:2–3_____

   _____

   _____

   _____

15. Your first priority in times of adversity should be to honor and glorify God by trusting Him, but you will tend to first seek relief from your feelings of sorrow, heartache, or disappointment. What comfort can you gain from the following verses?

   II Corinthians 12:9_____

   _____

   _____

   _____

   Philippians 4:6–7_____

   _____

   _____

   _____

16. During my first husband's illness and eventual death, I often prayed with a list of requests for his healing. God gave him the ultimate healing when he was taken to glory, but that was not what I had had in mind. I found in my desperation that I was dictating to God what He should be doing. Death changes every area of our lives, and the changes are not always welcome. Do you want God to direct your life, or are you dictating to Him? Read the following verses and write out their message to you today.

Psalm 46:10_____

_____

_____

Lamentations 3:25–26_____

_____

_____

Lamentations 3:32–40_____

_____

_____

_____

17. Looking back at Romans 8:28, what things do you see that could be good in the death of your loved one? List those here. Be honest with yourself and think through some of the verses already mentioned.

_____

_____

_____

_____

_____

_____

God has promised that He will work all things out for the good of those who love Him and keep His Word. Where do you see yourself in this? We cannot answer all the "why" questions or even most of them. Only God can! Fate or chance has nothing to do with the happenings in your life. A young couple whose son was killed in a shooting accident had been told by many that he was in the wrong place at the wrong time. Fate? Chance? No, it was God's direction and plan. This is hard to understand, but God is present in all your circumstances.

18. How does Lamentations 3:22–23 remind us of God's faithfulness?

_____

_____

_____

I live in a rural area where many roads lead to one destination. When I leave my driveway, I can turn left or right. Both roads take me to the same place. Sometimes we see our grief going down one road and our faith down another. Will the two ever meet? Yes, they can. There are many examples of people in Scripture that seemed to be heading down the wrong path, but observing with the knowledge we have today, we can see how the Lord led. Mary, the mother of Jesus, was pregnant without being married (Luke 1:26–35). Joseph was treated cruelly by his brothers (Genesis 37:12–28; 45:1–5).

God's voice may seem as though it is very much in the distance right now. It is somewhat like a child that whispers in your ear, but you cannot quite understand all the words.

Death does not come upon your loved one or you, the survivor, for punishment. You may not know the purpose God has in mind for His timing of a death, but you can claim Romans 8:29. He says in this verse that He (God) wants you (His child) to be conformed to His image (to be like Him, to have His will your will, for the good of your soul and not your body, for the eternal good rather then the good of the present). Your responsibility is to claim His Word and trust His leading.

19. Read Proverbs 3:5–6. How do you see yourself and your circumstances in light of these verses?

_____

_____

_____

20. How can you take comfort in the following verses?

I Peter 1:6–7_____

_____

_____

Psalm 119:71_____

_____

_____

Job 23:10_____

_____

_____

Lord,
Speak again, and I will try hard to listen. I want to hear everything You
have to say, repeatedly. Reassure me of Your love and constant care. Teach
me to trust You in all the circumstances of my life, the good times, as well as
the hard times. Assure my heart that You are in control, leading, guiding,
and directing my life day by day. Remind me of the promises in Your Word
that You are working a purpose in my life that I may not understand this
side of heaven. Help me to trust in Your love and goodness even when I do
not understand. Amen.

SEPARATION *lesson two*

*Y*ou have experienced a death in your family. The news might have come from a doctor, nurse, hospice worker, police, or family member. Or you might have been by the bedside of your loved one. When death occurs, we are aware that separation has taken place. As a Christian, we may think we will be removed from the many emotions that occur when death comes into our lives. We will look at some of these emotions later in our book, but for now let us see what the Scriptures have to say about us and how we are made.

1. Read Psalm 139:14. What does this verse say about us?

_____

_____

Because we are God's creation, and He has made each one of us unique, what does the beginning of verse 14 say we are to do?

_____

_____

2. Have you found this hard to do when in the midst of your grief?

_____

3. You are unique, and so was your loved one. List some ways your loved one was unique.

_____

_____

_____

_____

4. List some ways that you are different from your loved one.

_____

_____

_____

_____

5. Now list ways your relationship with your loved one was unique.

_____

_____

_____

_____

6. Read the following Scriptures. Identify the people in the verses and then give the unique relationship they had.

	People	Relationship
Genesis 2:20–24	_____	_____
	_____	_____
Ruth 1:11–18	_____	_____

	People	Relationship
I Samuel 18:1–4		
II Samuel 12:15–19		
John 11:1–5		

In many of the events you have just read about, someone died. A relationship was severed. Households were broken by death. We see the sadness and grief that the losses brought. Death reminds us that we have no control over life or death. This is also true when it comes to facing our grief. We may want to stop the world and get off. We may want people around us to stop their activities and realize the hurt and pain we are feeling. Death is a part of life. That grief follows death is normal.

Because you have easy access to God's Word, you may have been in Bible studies for years and claim a close relationship to the Lord. That does not shelter you from the grief that comes to your life as the result of death. Matthew 5:4 says, "Blessed are they that mourn: for they shall be comforted." Your grief should not be undermined or hurried along with quick fixes and answers from you, your family, or your friends. Grieving takes time and energy. It is not wrong to grieve after a significant loss. Your pain is not sin or weakness of faith. It is a normal, healthy response to loss. You will not begin to heal until you accept the rightfulness of your suffering over separation.

7. Explain how each of the following verses can be a comfort. Note those that you find hard to relate to and claim as your own right now.

Psalm 18:30 _____

_____

_____

_____

_____

Proverbs 3:5–6 _____

_____

_____

_____

_____

Isaiah 26:3 _____

_____

_____

_____

_____

Isaiah 40:31 _____

_____

_____

_____

_____

Isaiah 43:2 _____

_____

_____

_____

_____

Jeremiah 29:11_____

_____

_____

_____

_____

Look over the verses again and underline in your Bible those that you have claimed but need to be reminded of from time to time.

8. Read II Corinthians 4:16. Write out this verse in your own words, reminding yourself of the daily need for renewal in God's Word.

_____

_____

_____

_____

_____

9. With loss also comes change. Below are listed some changes that often come to the life of the one who has experienced a death. Check all that apply to you.

- Mealtimes
- Living quarters
- Shopping
- Finances
- Friends
- Church attendance
- Motivation
- Relationship to family
- Prayer and Bible reading
- Concentration
- Housekeeping
- Driving
- Feeling overwhelmed

10. List some changes you have experienced that may be different from those suggested above.

_____

_____

_____

_____

_____

11. Have you also noticed some changes in yourself physically?

- Sleeping pattern
- Diarrhea
- Appetite
- Headaches
- Memory lapses
- Muscle aches
- Panic attacks
- Dizziness
- Stomach cramps
- Sensitivity to noise or smell

12. List others you may have experienced that are not in the list above.

_____

_____

_____

_____

_____

Read Psalm 139:14 again. When considering the verses above, think about how we are put together in such a wonderful way. What does this have to do with grief? Some people may have the idea that if their faith is strong enough they should not experience the feelings of grief. Yes, we have the strength of the Lord to rely on, but we are still made with a physical and emotional body. We can still feel pain, emotionally and physically.

13. When facing grief, you may have wondered, "Does God still love me?" "How can I know God is near when I feel so far from Him?" "What can be done to lift this cloud of grief from off my shoulders?" "Why, God?" "Why now?" List some of the doubts you have had as a result of your loss.

_____

_____

_____

_____

14. Job probably suffered more than anyone else recorded in Scripture. He was so discouraged about his situation that he made three rash statements. Read these verses and write out his despairing statements in your own words.

Job 3:3a_____

_____

_____

Job 3:3b_____

_____

_____

Job 3:11_____

_____

_____

God called Job a righteous man and one that feared God. This should give us comfort when we feel that our grief is too much to bear.

15. How can the following verses be a comfort to you today?

Isaiah 40:31_____

_____

_____

_____

Isaiah 41:10_____

_____

_____

_____

Isaiah 55:8–9_____

_____

_____

_____

Jeremiah 10:23_____

_____

_____

_____

Romans 8:38–39_____

_____

_____

_____

A Very Present Help

He's helping me now—this moment,
Though I many not see it or hear,
Perhaps by a friend far distant,
Perhaps by a stranger near,
Perhaps by a spoken message,
Perhaps by the printed word;
In ways that I know and know not
I have the help of the Lord.

He's keeping me now—this moment,
However I need it most,
Perhaps by a single angel,
Perhaps by a mighty host,
Perhaps by the chain that frets me,
Or the walls that shut me in;
In ways that I know and know not
He keeps me from harm and sin.

He's guiding me now—this moment,
In pathways easy or hard,
Perhaps by a door wide open,
Perhaps by a door fast barred,
Perhaps by a joy withholden,
Perhaps by a gladness given;
In ways that I know and know not
He's leading me up to heaven.

He's using me now—this moment,
And whether I go or stand,
Perhaps by a plan accomplished,
Perhaps when he stays my hand,
Perhaps by a word in season,
Perhaps by a silent prayer;
In ways that I know and know not
His labor of love I share.

—*Annie Johnson Flint*

Heavenly Father,
I am thankful, O Lord, for You know my inner thoughts—the stress, agony,
despair, physical problems, separation, and loneliness I feel at this time. I
would ask You to give me Your strength, wisdom, peace, and comfort for
today and remind me that You are with me no matter what comes into my
life. Amen.

CHANGE
lesson three

When death has occurred, your life is changed. Sometimes the change is welcomed. That may sound strange when you have just finished a chapter on separation. We will look at the welcome changes, and then we will look at some changes that may not be welcomed. We will also look at what we can do about the changes that have resulted from the death of your husband or wife, mother or father, child, brother or sister, or other special person in your life.

During counseling, a young woman whose child had died after a lingering illness said to me that she welcomed the death but dreaded the days, weeks, and months ahead. The death of someone who has suffered for many weeks or even years can bring a feeling of relief to you.

1. Read Psalm 116:15. What is the first word in this verse? Look up the word in a dictionary and write out the definition that the psalmist is using.

   _____

   _____

2. Two people are mentioned in this verse. Name those two people.

_____

Did you ever think that the Lord counts it as precious when one of His children dies? Read Psalm 23. The psalmist says that death is only a shadow. A shadow is temporary and it cannot cause harm.

3. Why do you think the death of a "saint" is precious in the sight of the Lord?

_____

_____

_____

4. Read II Corinthians 5:6–8. According to verse 8, where is someone abiding when he or she is absent from this body?

_____

The presence of the Lord must be a wonderful place. In the prayer that Jesus taught His disciples He said, "Our Father, who art in heaven." God has prepared heaven—no more trials, pain, sickness, cares of this world, anxieties, or worries.

5. According to Revelation 21:4, your loved one is no longer burdened with the cares of this world. List some of the cares that have been very real to you and your loved one in the past days, weeks, or months. Can you thank God right now that your loved one is not facing those cares anymore?

_____

_____

_____

_____

_____

_____

6. The question is often asked, "Will my loved one know me in heaven?" First Corinthians 13:12 speaks of this. What assurance can you find in this verse?

_____

I have mentioned the comforting fact that your loved one is in the presence of the Lord. This can bring you comfort, but it does not remove the change that has to come into your life. You may resist change.

7. Once again, I want you to look at a checklist. Some of these items are repeated from the previous chapter. What has changed in your life since your loved one died?

- Sleeping pattern

- Eating habits

- Housework

- Friendships

- Financial responsibility

- Transportation

- Vacation

- Housing

- Lawn and yard care

- Church attendance

- Family times

- Interests or hobbies

- Home repairs

- Reading

- Concentration

- Clubs or organizations

Many do not realize the impact a death has on a family until they make a list of those changes. Some of the things listed above may be new to you, possible areas where you will need help and instruction.

8. James 1:5 tells where to start when you are seeking help. Where should your first request be directed?

_____

Begin by making a list of your needs. Focus on one area at a time. Seek counsel from those who can be trusted to give you sound advice. This help can come from family, friends, pastors, professionals (attorney, financial advisor, counselor), other widows or widowers, and so forth.

9. When you have sought the wisdom of the Lord mentioned in James 1:5, you are to continue to earnestly look to Him for help and guidance. Proverbs 3:5–6 gives a caution that you should heed. What is this caution?

_____

10. The book of Job is a clear picture of a man who suffered. Read Job 1:13–19 and list the losses Job suffered. In all of Job's suffering and losses, what does verse 22 tell about Job?

_____

_____

_____

11. Look at Job's support team through all his phases of suffering. The one who should have been the most encouraging to him was not. Who is speaking in Job 2:9? What does this verse suggest?

_____

_____

You may have been disappointed in your support team. Sometimes those that are the closest to you are not your best cheerleaders.

12. What do you expect from your support team?

_____

_____

_____

I was recently talking with someone whose father-in-law had died three months earlier. In talking with her, I asked about her mother-in-law. She said that her mother-in-law still cried, was disorganized, and was not interested in life's activities. Then she added, "She should be over this by now." How unreasonable can one be? Someone with whom the mother-in-law had shared fifty plus years, planned together, raised a family together, saved for hard times, laughed through good times, could hardly be expected to be back to normal in three months. What is normal? Your life has been forever changed by the death and will never be as it was before. This is not to say your life will never have meaning or be enjoyable again, but your life has changed forever.

13. Most of the book of Job is a dialogue between Job and three of his friends concerning the cause of Job's suffering. Read Job 2:11. Name Job's three friends. Why had they come to see Job?

_____

_____

Job's three friends assumed that his suffering was a direct result of sin. They told Job that if he would only repent, everything would be all right. How wrong they were. Losses are not always a direct result of personal sin. Do not add feelings of guilt to your grief. When you look closely at Job 3–31, you see a lot of talking rather than comforting.

In Job 32, a young man entered the picture and suggested that God was punishing Job in order to humble him. This was partially true. When you are faced with trials, by death or other testing, they can purify your faith. You do not know the mind of God in the trials of suffering. Your part is to trust and be faithful.

How can you be faithful to God when you feel that you have been wronged or that God seems uncaring or that His timing is off and you are hurting so badly? The following verses can comfort you and strengthen your faith.

14. Read the following verses, and then answer the questions.

Psalm 33:21—Can your heart rejoice even in the hard times? Why or why not? Where is your trust? Friends? Bank account? Possessions? Family? Your job? Doctors? Personal goals?

_____

_____

_____

Psalm 27:14—What do you think it means to "wait on the Lord"? Do you find waiting hard? Explain.

_____

_____

_____

II Timothy 1:7—Your mind plays tricks on you during the time of trials—doubting, questioning, searching, and longing for the past—but in II Timothy 1:7 God has promised you power, love, and a sound mind. How can these gifts be uplifting to you right now?

_____

_____

_____

15 Read Psalm 27:1–6 to see the faith that David showed. This psalm mentions fear a number of times. List some of the fears David had.

_____

_____

16. David concluded Psalm 27:14 with encouragement to wait on the Lord. David gives another command and a promise. What is the command? What is the promise?

_____

_____

Wait for God's plans for the future. Wait for God to supply needs. Wait for the encouragement you can receive from God's Word. Wait for the comfort God will provide.

Lord,

You are the only One Who knows all the changes that have come into my life because of this death. I ask that You will lead and guide me through these changes. Give me wisdom for decisions I need to make. Give me the strength to make the changes that need to be made. I know You are a God Who does not change. Amen.

ANGER
lesson four

*M*any Christians question the depth of their grieving. Some even teach that Christians should not grieve or feel sad and lonely because we have the God of all comfort (II Corinthians 1:3–5). Yes, God is the God of all comfort and how thankful you can be for that. But if you did not need comforting, He would not have mentioned that He is the God of all comfort. You were created with emotions, which allow you to feel the reality of your hurts and the depth of the relief your Father brings. Some of the emotions that are felt at the time of loss may include the following.

Fear	Bewilderment	Panic
Anger	Frustration	Inability to function
Regret	Loneliness	Bitterness
Guilt	Depression	Lack of concentration
Uselessness	Physical distress	No motivation to live
Displacement	Resentment	Desire to die

A desire to return to "normal" can bring a great deal of pressure to your life. That pressure should not come between you and the Lord. It should draw you closer to Him. Learning to walk in your grief makes you aware of the presence of God (II Corinthians 5:7). How helpless you are without His constant care and loving concern. During this time you can often be less patient with others and yourself, yet you should learn to be less judgmental. The fire of trials often burns away the wood, hay, and stubble in our lives and makes us more like the Master, stripping away our arrogance. Someone once said, "Trials will make you bitter or better."

1. Why do you think God made you with emotions?

   _____

   _____

   _____

2. What do you think life would be like without emotions?

   _____

   _____

   _____

In this chapter we will study the emotion of anger. Used in the wrong way, anger is not biblical but can be a real part of grieving.

3. Have you experienced anger since your loved one died or even before the death? In my counseling experience, I have found that other people may cause anger during your grieving. Look over the list and check any that apply to you.

   - The deceased

   - The doctor

   - The hospital

   - Church members

   - Friends

- Rescue squad
- Your children
- In-laws
- Stepfamily
- Yourself
- The pastor
- Neighbors

Let's take a look at anger and what the Bible has to say about it.

4. Look up the word *anger* in the dictionary and write out the definition.

_____

_____

_____

_____

The basic meaning is displeasure or hostility. You are displeased with your circumstances at this time. God is not mentioned in the previous list. You are angry with God because you know He controls life and death.

5. Read the following verses and identify who was angry and why. Note the person and the reason.

Genesis 30:1–3

Who_____

_____

Why_____

_____

Psalm 38:3

Who_____

_____

Why_____

_____

Proverbs 15:1

Who_____

_____

Why_____

_____

Daniel 2:10–13

Who_____

_____

Why_____

_____

Jonah 3:5–4:1

Who_____

_____

Why_____

_____

6. What does the Bible say about anger in the following verses?

Proverbs 15:1_____

_____

_____

Ecclesiastes 7:9_____

_____

_____

Matthew 5:22_____

_____

_____

7. Read Ephesians 4:26. What does this verse say about anger?

_____

_____

Does this mean it is all right to be angry? No. The wrong kind of anger keeps you awake at night. It is the anger that breaks your fellowship with God and your family and friends. You should handle anger properly. Anger vented thoughtlessly can hurt others and destroy fellowship with God and people. If bottled up inside, it can cause you to become bitter. It will destroy you from within. If you nurse your anger, you will give Satan a foothold. You need to settle your feelings of anger. This may mean going to someone with a heart of love or going to the Lord with a repentant heart.

8. How can Job 23:10, 14 apply to anger?

_____

_____

You have to look at anger as part of your grief. We have seen that the Lord is not pleased with your anger. But let us see more about anger.

9. Sometimes anger is displayed in your conversation. Have you been sarcastic in your conversation? Read Ephesians 4:29. What does this verse say about how you speak in dealing with other people?

_____

_____

10. The book of James has a lot to say about the use of the tongue. Read James 3:7–14. What does James say about your heart and the tongue in verse 10?

_____

_____

_____

11. Do you have the attitude that you are right and everyone else is wrong? Do you believe that you have the right to be angry? Read Romans 12:3. Is it hard to look at yourself and see where you could be wrong? Explain.

_____

_____

_____

12. Anger can be displayed in your actions. Read Exodus 32:19–20. Who was angry? Why was he angry?

_____

_____

_____

Moses was angry not only with the children of Israel but also with Aaron their leader. I have known widows and widowers who were so angry that they changed their will, made decisions too quickly, and later regretted what had been done. Never make decisions when you are angry.

13. Read Romans 12:2. How can you apply this to your decision making?

_____

_____

_____

14. What are you commanded to do in Colossians 3:8–9?

_____

_____

15. What are the commands of Colossians 3:10?

_____

_____

As we have seen, expressions of anger are real. They can bring destruction, hurt, loss, sleeplessness, and even physical problems. The solution to anger is to see what God has to say about it, to see how He would respond to anger. Romans 12:2 says that you can have a renewed mind, but this can happen only when you respond in the right way to God and His Word.

16. Often we want to demand that someone else change or that our circumstances change rather than accept God's sovereign choices in our lives. Death has been one of those choices that God has brought about at this time. You may not understand His ways or His thinking. Read Isaiah 55:8–9. How can these verses be a comfort to you when you are angry?

_____

_____

_____

_____

17. Read Psalm 94:11. This verse says our thoughts are vanity or empty. They are not God's thoughts. Have you had some empty, vain, or angry thoughts?

_____

_____

_____

18. A verse to memorize and claim in this time of grief and anger is Proverbs 16:3. Write it out here.

_____

_____

_____

_____

God will help you each day to commit your works to Him and then He will direct your thoughts. Here are some beliefs grieving people often have about anger:

> No matter who gets hurt, I should get what
> I want. I will do anything to get it.

> I should avoid distress at all costs. I must
> never be uncomfortable or frustrated.

> I have a right to be angry with others. They have hurt
> my feelings, caused me discomfort, or disappointed me.

> I have a right to be irritable and
> others should leave me alone.

19. Do you think the beliefs mentioned above are godly thoughts or fleshly thoughts? Explain.

_____

_____

These thoughts are damaging to your relationship with the Lord and others.

20. Explain how Proverbs 16:3 can apply to your situation when you are angry.

_____

_____

Heavenly Father,

Thank You, Lord, for Your constant patience with me, loving me when I am unlovely, showing me Your Word, which has all the answers to life's problems. Help me to apply what I have read and learned. In Your lovely and faithful name I pray. Amen.

WHEN THE BIBLE IS SILENT
lesson five

*E*ven though there are many facets of grief that the Bible does not address, there are principles in God's Word to give you guidance when you have to make decisions. Many times these aspects of grieving are the ones you struggle with most. It may seem that your grieving is a no-win situation. No matter what decisions you make, someone will have a contrary comment or suggestion. A few are discussed here. Think of other decisions you have faced.

Wedding rings. Does Scripture address the issue of taking off your wedding ring? No! When is the best time to remove it? Should you take it off at all? What do you do with it after you have removed it? This should be a personal decision. It should not matter to anyone else, nor should it be his or her concern. In dealing with many widows and widowers over the years, I have seen some leave their ring on permanently. No question about removing it ever entered their mind.

Some still feel married, and the ring stays on. In the public eye, some want to appear married, so they leave their ring on. Others have removed their ring the day after the funeral. Others have moved their wedding ring from the left hand to the right hand. If this is the case, when does the ring go on the other hand? Many people think ahead and decide on a certain date when the ring will change hands.

One factor to consider in this is the question of dating again (more about this in the chapter "Moving On"). If you would like to date again, then it would be natural either to remove the ring or to put it on the right hand. Men often remove their wedding band sooner than women.

Clothing. Another issue that often comes up is cleaning out clothing and other possessions. Again, this is a personal decision. May I offer a few suggestions that may be helpful? For the first few weeks after the funeral, many people are so numb that decisions can be made too quickly. I know several people whose children or close friend cleaned out clothing and possessions as soon as the funeral was over. The widow or widower often felt robbed and wished a little more time had elapsed before doing this very personal task.

Personal items. Then the question comes of what to do with personal items. Once again, this should be your decision, but you can be open to suggestions from others. Make no commitments when your emotions are high and you cannot make clear decisions. Those things are yours now and should not be taken away until you give them away.

First, offer things to your children, grandchildren, brothers, sisters, and close friends. It is often surprising what significance people place on things. When my first husband died, I offered to give to the grandchildren what they wanted. The oldest grandchild wanted her granddad's shoehorn. A shoehorn? I asked her why. She remembered him showing her how to use it while sitting on our sofa one Sunday morning before church. I would never have thought to give it to her unless she had asked.

If the death involves stepchildren, consider their feelings and attachment to items. Some of the things they treasure may have family attachment and these should stay in their family. Remember you are dealing with things, and these will some day be left behind by all of us. Family relationships are more important than the things that divide us.

Consider needy families in your community when you are disposing of items. Be aware of other people's needs and offer to give what you can spare. Be sure to give with an open hand, remembering that the item may not have the same meaning to those receiving it as it does to you. You may see that expensive sweater some weeks later with dirt on it or wrinkled and snagged.

Throw some things away. We all collect things that have no value now or in the future. Be willing to get rid of the clutter in your home. Clutter often brings confusion, depression, and disorganization.

Save some items that you have strong attachment to and have been meaningful to you as a couple through the years. If you are a woman and can wear some of your husband's clothes, then save them. Your husband's flannel shirt will feel good in the winter as an extra covering. Pictures are another focal point for both men and women.

Downsizing. Widows and widowers usually begin to think of downsizing. You may have already moved, and along with that, you probably have downsized. This can be a very dramatic change for you and for your family. There can be many reasons to downsize.

- Finances
- Convenience
- Family closeness
- Health
- Home maintenance
- Yard maintenance
- Security
- Transportation
- Retirement home with activities
- Retirement home with meals provided

When you begin to think of downsizing, you wonder what to do with all that you have collected over the years. Do not despair. You, and thousands like you, have made a move. Moving does not mean you are giving up a sense of home. Take your treasures. The big decisions come when you try to decide what to keep, what to give away, or what to throw away.

First, choose something that will fit your needs and budget and not what others might suggest. Listen to their suggestions and reasoning, but you are the one to make the final decision.

Look for a house or apartment that will last you the rest of your days. Are the door openings wide enough for a wheelchair? Is everything on one floor? Are doctors and hospitals close by? What about security? Will you feel safe in your new location? Choose a place with plenty of light, large closets, and extra storage space, if needed. If you are interested in activities, are there some close by or provided by the place you are moving to?

Now, how do you downsize? This can be liberating but also difficult. Decide what things really matter to you. If you have a set of china that has been boxed up in a closet for twenty-five years, you can probably do without it, even if it has been in the family for years. Always consider family photographs. Take useful and functional items. Keep meaningful things.

Ask your children to take their possessions to their own homes. Often when you downsize, large pieces of furniture do not fit. Look at each piece of furniture and decide if it will serve another need in your new location. Sort through your hobbies for those you will continue and for those that are no longer of interest. Unload what you do not want; keep what you do want.

Some of your precious possessions can be divided among family members, special friends, or others who would appreciate them. Some of these items may be sold at auction or an estate sale. You can donate some things to charity and claim a tax deduction.

Once you decide where you are moving, count the rooms you now have and the rooms you will have. Look at the floor plan and wall space, and calculate square footage. The rooms may be designated living room, dining room, bedroom, or kitchen, but you do not have to use them that way. The kitchen may also be used as a craft room; the dining room may become the library. Be open to suggestions and try to be creative. You may move into half the space you are used to, but you will soon be comfortable with less stuff.

When the time comes to move, get a professional to help with the actual move. There will be the potential for less damage, and the responsibility will not be with family members or friends offering their help. Think of the move as a new adventure, an opportunity to learn and grow.

Money. Many who have not handled the family finances find this task to be overwhelming at times. Seek help from your financial institution, your stockbroker, your children, or other resources you trust. Do not take just anyone into your confidence. Beware of telemarketers. Many widows and widowers get themselves in financial trouble because of a smooth talker. It may take a year to understand where you stand financially. Be patient with insurance companies and other institutions. When making calls to these organizations, keep good records of the phone number you call, the date you call, and to whom you speak. Your mind may be very fuzzy during the early bereavement period, so keeping good records will give you peace of mind. If you have not previously handled the finances, it will take time to become comfortable with making decisions and knowing where you stand financially. Remember not to overspend in an attempt to buy away your grief.

Legal matters. Now is the time to have a will drawn up or to make changes to your current will, to have a medical directive drawn up for yourself, and to make your own funeral arrangements. Once again, input from your children or a trusted friend will be helpful. I was advised not to put my children on the deed to my house or to own property jointly. This was not because I do not trust my children, but if an accident occurred and I was sued, my children and I could lose everything we own. You may look into living trusts. These are legal papers, so know what you are signing. Make a list of all the legal papers someone will need at your time of death. Give a copy of these papers to your power of attorney, your lawyer, or the executor of your will. If you have a safe deposit box at the bank, be sure this person knows where the key is. If you use a computer for keeping records, record somewhere what your password is so those needing to enter your computer for legal information can do so.

Dining alone. Many find that eating alone is one of the hardest things to do. Women are used to cooking for their husband and often cooked to please him. Now for whom do they cook? Many men are lost in the kitchen, but a few enjoy cooking. Some have had to cook over the years because of necessity. There is a freedom in being a widow or a widower when it comes to eating. You can fix what you want, when you want, and how much you want. You can even eat anywhere you want, if you care to do that. The bottom line is to eat a good balanced meal and take care of yourself. Eating with a friend at a local restaurant can be enjoyable. The budget may not often allow for this, but look for those opportunities.

Silly stuff. I use this term because of one of the opening statements I made: "Grieving is a no-win situation." If you move, people will watch and question what you do. If you buy a new car, you are spending someone's inheritance. If you keep the old car, then you cannot part with the old clunker because of sentimental reasons. If you change your hairstyle, you are trying to gain attention. If you keep the same hairstyle, some will wonder why you do not get up to date with the rest of the world. I could mention other 'no-win situations,' but just be aware that they are out there. You need to do what you feel the Lord wants you do in making decisions.

As I mentioned at the beginning of this chapter, I have found Scripture verses that can give guidelines in many of the areas we have mentioned.

Read Psalm 34 to answer the following questions. Be sure to keep in mind the principles that have been discussed in this chapter.

1. Even in your decision making, what should be your goal according to Psalm 34:1, 3?

    _____

    _____

2. According to Psalm 34:4, in any decision you have to make, what should be the first thing you do?

    _____

3. This verse also makes a promise that you can claim. What is that promise?

    _____

    _____

4. Psalm 34:7 says that you are not alone at any time. Who is there to be with you?

    _____

5. As a person who is hurting, you may use your tongue in the wrong manner. What does verse 13 warn you about?

    _____

    _____

6. Look up the word *guile* in a dictionary. Write out the meaning here.

    _____

    _____

7. How does this relate to your grieving experience or decision making?

    _____

    _____

8. We are told in verse 14 to depart from evil and seek peace. Have you tried to do this in your decision making? Explain.

_____

_____

_____

_____

9. Verse 15 says that the eyes of the Lord are upon the righteous and His ears are open unto their cry. Have you been aware of the Lord's presence and His watchful eye as you have made decisions that were misunderstood? Explain.

_____

_____

_____

_____

10. Verse 18 can be a source of great comfort in times of grief. What are the characteristics of the heart and spirit in this verse?

_____

_____

11. The word *contrite* in this verse also means "crushed spirit." Have you felt that your spirit has been crushed as you made some of the decisions that were mentioned in this chapter?

_____

There is a great promise in verse 22. Have you thought about the fact that the God of the universe loves you enough to redeem your soul? The word *redeem* in this verse is the idea of setting free. God has promised to set your soul, or spirit, free from the bondage that you may feel you are under. Have you let God's Spirit set you free from the talk and opinions of others? Pray and ask His Spirit to do that for you right now.

Jesus Whispers Peace

There is a name to me so dear,
Like sweetest music to my ear;
For when my heart is troubled, filled with fear,
Jesus whispers peace.
When grief seems more than I can bear,
My soul weighed down with heavy care;
And I am sorely tempted to despair,
Jesus whispers peace.
O, that the world might hear Him speak,
The word of comfort that men seek;
To all the lowly, and unto the meek,
Jesus whispers peace.

—*Della McClain Warren*

Lord,
You have promised us wisdom if we ask for it. In this area of decision making I ask that You give me the wisdom I need to make the right decisions. I pray for an "open hand" in the tough decision of wanting to hold on to earthly possessions. I realize these will one day all be left behind. Give patience, understanding, and wisdom if there is conflict. Help me to feel your presence even with these changes in my life. Amen.

LONELY VS. ALONE VS. LONELY

*I*n the many years I have counseled people following the death of a loved one, one common thread runs through their grief—they feel alone. If you look up the words *alone* or *loneliness* in a dictionary, you find the definition "solitary, lack of intimacy, apart from someone or something." The word *alone* is used many times in Scripture, but the word *lonely* is not found.

What are the differences between being alone and being lonely?

1. Can a Christian ever feel alone?

   _____

2. According to Genesis 2:7–8, 20 who was the first person to be alone? According to Genesis 2:18 who recognized that Adam was alone?

   _____

3. We have already seen that Adam was alone, but there are other examples in the Bible of people feeling alone. Read the following references to see who felt alone.

I Kings 19:1–4, 14_____

_____

Psalm 102:1–11_____

_____

Matthew 14:23_____

_____

I Thessalonians 3:1–3_____

_____

These examples are of godly men who in times of testing felt very alone. The circumstances and reasons for their loneliness varied, but loneliness or aloneness was the common emotion with each one. Man has a basic need—fellowship with other people and with God. The source for filling that need is God. In every heart there is a God-created vacuum for fellowship with Him.

4. Where does this fellowship start? Read the following verses to see how you can have fellowship with God. Write out these verses in your own words.

Romans 5:8_____

_____

_____

_____

Ephesians 2:8–9_____

_____

_____

_____

If you have not already accepted this fellowship through Christ, will you now accept Christ as your personal Savior? You need to realize that you cannot have perfect fellowship with God without first knowing His Son, Jesus Christ, as your personal Savior.

5. Many who are using this Bible study have already accepted Christ as Savior but still face human loneliness because their loved one is gone. Many are living alone for the first time in their lives. Is loneliness in the life of a Christian a possibility? Explain.

_____

_____

_____

6. The word *alone* in the Bible does not always refer to loneliness. Read John 16:32. Who was speaking in this verse? Whom did He say was with Him?

_____

_____

How can you take comfort in the fact that Christ is with you?

_____

_____

7. Read Psalm 142 in relationship to your being alone. According to verse 1 whom did David cry out to? Have you done that?

_____

8. According to verse 2 what did David do before the Lord? Have you done that?

_____

9. According to verse 3 how did David describe his spirit? Who knew his path even in his feelings?

_____

10. According to verse 4 David made several statements about his plight. Write out his statements in your own words. Have you felt that people have not understood the depth of your loss? Explain.

_____

_____

_____

_____

11. David said two important things about God in verse 5. What are they?

_____

_____

Have you found God to be a refuge and your portion as you continue to adjust to your loss?

_____

David mentioned his persecutors in verse 6. We need to be careful that we know who our "persecutors" are while we are grieving. I have found there are not many real persecutors but many imaginary ones. In verse 7 David asked that his soul be let out of prison. Why did he want to feel better?

Praise is a wonderful way to be released from the feelings of loneliness and aloneness.

I mentioned to a Christian friend that I was writing this book. She has been a widow for many years. I asked her what suggestion she would have for a chapter. She responded, "Write a chapter on blessings." That really surprised me, but when we think about the blessings that God has given to us, we could each write our own book.

12. Solitude is not always loneliness, and solitude can be healing in the time of grieving. Loneliness can be a negative experience, but solitude can be positive. We have an example in Scripture of a time

our Lord wanted to be alone. Read Mark 1:35. What was the purpose of Jesus' wanting to be alone?

_____

_____

_____

I have found that my times alone in Bible reading and prayer have been very rewarding and fulfilling. Do you take time each day to get alone with the Lord for your time of solitude?

During the grieving process, many are often physically and emotionally weak. Your times of quiet solitude can be times of refreshment and enjoyment. In these times of solitude, you are faced with your own thoughts and feelings. Maybe this is why you do not like being alone. Read the following verses to see where you should focus your thoughts.

13. Read Psalm 73:26. How have you seen God's strength during these days of adjustment?

_____

_____

_____

14. Read Psalm 118. God is good even when you cannot see what He is doing in your life. Give one recent example of His goodness to you.

_____

_____

_____

According to Isaiah 26:3 God has perfect peace for you. My late husband once said, "Don't look at the past, the future, those around you, or other people. Look to the Lord for your perfect peace."

15. Read Jeremiah 29:11. God is thinking about you. Is this verse a comfort to you? Explain.

_____

_____

_____

16. Read Lamentations 3:22–25. God is faithful. Are you looking for His new mercies every day?

_____

God's promises must be claimed by faith. As you read God's Word, look for passages that speak to your heart and memorize these verses so that you can recall them in times of loneliness.

I have expressed many times that I am lonely because I want someone to hold, someone with skin on. We feel God's presence and know His promises, but still the feelings of loneliness can be overwhelming. Is this wrong? Are these feelings sinful? I do not believe they are.

17. Answer the following questions to get a perspective on your loneliness.

a. How long did you know this person?

_____

b. Have you lived alone before?

_____

c. Do you have other family members living close by?

_____

d. Are they in touch as often as you would like?

_____

e. Are you involved with other people on a social basis?

_____

f. Are you involved in a church that provides times of fellowship?

_____

g. Do you take advantage of these times?

_____

h. Do you have financial problems?

_____

i. Are you a shy person?

_____

j. Are you often bored?

_____

k. Do you reach out to other people?

_____

l. Is your health good?

_____

m. Do you sleep well at night?

_____

n. Do you have hobbies?

_____

o. Do you have a pet?

_____

p. Are there others you can share a meal with?

_____

q. Can you drive?

_____

r. Do you have to do household chores that you are not familiar with?

_____

s. Did you and your loved one do things primarily together?

_____

t. Do you include other people in your plans?

_____

u. Do you look for humor in everyday happenings?

_____

v. Do you make plans for each day?

_____

w. Do you look for opportunities to be with other people?

_____

Some of these questions focus on the negative idea. Focus instead on the positive. Many times your identity was one with the person who has died. When my first husband died, I grieved as much for the ministry that we shared as I grieved for him. Many feel alone because they no longer feel like a couple.

18. Read II Corinthians 1:3–4. These are classic verses that many people read at the time of death. Who is the person of all comfort, even in loneliness? Why does He comfort us?

_____

_____

_____

Have you tried to reach out to other people who are hurting? Get involved in church activities, scan the local newspaper for clubs for hobby interests, volunteer at the library or hospital, be a tutor for children who need help, or read a book to a blind person. Seek contact with live people rather than whiling away hours in computer chat rooms or even on-line dating services. Many times your loneliness is a result of withdrawing from people for one reason or another. In addition to seeking the presence of the Lord, seek the fellowship and opportunity to be with other people. Widows and widowers are not the only ones that are hurting from loneliness. Have you ever thought of a child as being lonely? A teenager? A single mother? Another single lady or man?

19. Name some people around you that you see as being lonely. List some ways that you can reach out to them and be a comfort to them even in your loneliness.

_____

_____

_____

_____

Matthew 6:19–20 tells us to lay up treasures in heaven. Can you see how helping someone else who is lonely is laying up treasures for yourself?

20. How does II Corinthians 9:6 apply to being lonely?

_____

_____

_____

_____

When you are lonely, call someone you think might be lonely. Try to cheer her up and you will in turn be blessed. You need to get out of yourself, your little world, your selfish thoughts, and the pity party in which you often find yourself. Does it happen? Yes, to all of us. Read Philippians 4:8 and apply it each day.

Lord,

I come to You with a heart that is full of gratitude for the many blessings that You have given me. I thank You for friends that have reached out to me in my time of being alone. I am thankful for those that You have put across my path that I can help. Help me to focus on Your goodness and blessings and not on the aloneness and loneliness I feel. Amen.

GRIEF AND THE SHEPHERD
lesson seven

*I*s there a psalm that is better known than the Twenty-third Psalm? Many have memorized it, written about it, and preached hundreds of funerals focused on its meaning. The truths found in this psalm are easy to understand and yet hard to put into practice when we are faced with the death of a loved one. Let's see what David says and then how we can pray this psalm back to God for assurance and peace.

1. Look in your dictionary for the meaning of the word *shepherd* and write the definition here.

_____

_____

_____

My dictionary gives the meaning "one who guides sheep." Are we sheep? In the natural, physical sense, we are not, but God calls us sheep in the Scripture. I wonder why? When my first husband was a pastor, we had an opportunity to visit a farmer who raised sheep. We found out a lot about sheep on that visit and noted how we as people are so much like them. Let us look at some characteristics of sheep.

They are dumb animals. They cannot be trained to jump through hoops, pull a cart, or even swim in a creek. I think of this in my experience with my grieving. How could I be so dumb to doubt God's many promises? Yet repeatedly, I forget what He has told me for years. Here are a few verses of promise that you should examine and claim.

2. Read Proverbs 3:5–6. Do you trust the Lord with all your heart?

_____

3. Do you lean on your own understanding? Explain.

_____

_____

_____

_____

4. What happens when you do not acknowledge Him in all your ways?

_____

_____

_____

_____

5. What is the promise in this verse if you trust Him, lean on His understanding, and acknowledge Him? Are you willing to let Him direct you?

_____

_____

Read Joshua 1:9. This is a verse with a command. You are to be strong. Have you heard people say, "You'll do just fine. You are a strong person"? I have heard that comment many times. Do they mean strong physically, mentally, emotionally, or spiritually? Many times, I will admit that I do not feel strong in any of those areas, and yet God has commanded strength of us. He also tells us to be of good courage, not to be afraid and not to be dismayed.

6. Look up the word *dismayed* in a dictionary and write the definition here.

_____

_____

_____

How does God expect you to not feel frightened, discouraged, or troubled at a time like this? Look back at Joshua 1:9. God begins this verse with a question, "Have not I commanded thee?" This was not the first time God had told Joshua or the children of Israel to be strong, to trust, and not to be afraid or frightened. God had said this many times.

7. Why did He have to remind Joshua, and why does He have to remind you of His abiding presence? Were the children of Israel "dumb" sheep?

_____

_____

_____

Sheep are also dirty. It is the shepherd's job to keep his sheep clean. As they are grazing, briars, twigs, mud, and many things get entangled in their wool. After my first husband died, I got "entangled" with things that were not immoral but things that made me "dirty." Running was one of those entanglements. I asked myself why I was running all the time—running to work, running to the store, running to shop, running out to dinner—run, run, run. There is a difference between keeping busy and running. You run to keep your pain from catching up with you. That does not work. Maybe when you are still, you feel the pain of your loss more intensely.

8. Read Psalm 46:10. What does this verse tell you to do?

_____

_____

When you are still before the Lord, you are able to know God in a closer way and allow Him to draw you close to His heart. God can more easily handle your pain.

I also found myself withdrawing. Once again, this was defense against the pain. When you withdraw from other people and activities, you should seek the reason for withdrawal. It can be a time of reflection, of quiet study, of doing projects that need to be completed, or one of many other things. Then again this withdrawing can be a form of despondency.

9. Read James 4:8. Who desires your fellowship?

_____

Elijah needed a time alone after his battle with Ahab and Jezebel (I Kings 18:17–40). After his conflict with them, we find him running for his life.

10. Read I Kings 19:8–12. How did the Lord speak to Elijah?

_____

Your time spent alone with the Lord can strengthen you physically, emotionally, and spiritually.

11. In Matthew 14:23, the Lord was withdrawing from the crowd. What did He do when He withdrew?

_____

Another area that I saw as dirty was having a combative spirit or being argumentative. This was not my personality, and I knew it did not honor the Lord. When I focused on Philippians 4:8, my spirit was refreshed. When you have a combative spirit, this verse will help you refocus your thoughts.

Sheep are also defenseless. Sheep have no way of defending themselves from attack, but you have the best Shepherd to defend and protect you. Let us look at our Shepherd. Psalm 23:1 says, "The Lord is my shepherd, I shall not want." Who is your shepherd? Until death came, your "shepherd" may have been your spouse, success, money, or fame. You may be grieving not only for the one you lost but also the secondary losses you have faced. It could be loss of position, money, couple identity, or any number of things.

12. Are there secondary losses in your life? Name some of them.

_____

_____

Psalm 23:2 says, "He leadeth me beside the still waters." Your Shepherd will not drive you, but He wants to lead you.

13. Are you worried about the future? He is already there. Read Proverbs 16:9. Who will direct your steps if you let Him lead?

_____

The second part of Psalm 23:2 tells something else about our Lord's leading. He will lead "beside the still waters." Sheep will not drink from a running stream. I am told that if a sheep falls into water, his heavy wool coat will quickly absorb water and he will drown.

According to Mark 4:39 Jesus was able to still the stormy sea. In Mark 4:41 the disciples were surprised that even the wind and sea obey the Master. Will you let Him lead you beside the quiet waters and still your storm?

14. Psalm 23:3 says the Shepherd will provide restoration. Why would He give you restoration?

_____

Every night a shepherd gathers his sheep back into his barn or a corral for a night of rest. We, like sheep, need the restoration that rest and sleep can bring. Read Psalm 130. Memorize this psalm for rest and restoration.

15. Psalm 23:4 tells of two items the shepherd always has with him. What are they?

_____

I live in the country, and on a moonless night we have total darkness. My home is in the middle of several hundreds of acres. I would not walk anywhere outside after dark without a light to guide me to keep me from falling. Even when walking during the day, my husband carried his walking stick. He used this as a form of protection and assurance. Sheep have reasons to be afraid. They are defenseless. You need a heavenly Shepherd just as sheep need a physical shepherd.

When you have lost a loved one, you are in a deep, dark valley. You may not like the dark. It makes you feel uncertain of the way. Just as my husband carried his walking stick, our Shepherd carries His rod and staff. The comfort does not come from the rod and staff but from the One Who carries the rod and staff. You do not have to be afraid of the present or the future when you know the Shepherd Who carries the rod and staff.

16. Psalm 23:5 tells of the Shepherd's provision. What does the first part of verse 5 tell you? Who is surrounding that table?

_____

_____

Some of those you feel are your enemies may be real people. But your enemies may be Satan's attack on your peace of mind or may be lack of trust in the One Who has promised to supply all your needs.

17. Read Philippians 4:19. What is the promise in this verse?

_____

_____

Your spouse or parent provided for you, and now he or she is not here. You have anxious moments about your daily or monthly needs. Think back on other times in your life when you were anxious about your daily needs.

18. Read Matthew 6:25–34. What has God promised to do?

_____

_____

David ends Psalm 23:5 with praise to the Shepherd, Who knows how to supply each need. He is the good Shepherd, Who cannot fail.

19. Psalm 23:6 demonstrates a spirit of contentment. What assurance did David show?

_____

_____

David used two words at the beginning of verse 6 that someone has called twin sisters, "goodness and mercy." God is too wise not to be good and too loving not to show mercy. As you think of the days and weeks ahead, as you make your journey with grief, keep in mind the goodness and mercy of God. His goodness and mercy are not just for the weeks and months ahead but much longer than that.

Do you know many people who are content today? The death of your loved one may have brought a spirit of discontentment. Death means change, and change often brings restless feelings. How long will God's goodness and mercy last according to Psalm 23:6? That is a long time.

> Lord,
>
> Help me each day to feel Your presence, to know Your leading, and to trust You as my good and great Shepherd. Thank You for guidance, protection, goodness and provision. In times of doubt, bring verses of assurance to my mind. Above all, let me not forget to praise You for what You have done. You are a great God. Amen.

FEAR
lesson eight

*Y*ou are now alone! In chapter 6, we talked about loneliness and being lonely. These are real emotions, but fear is another emotion that many feel. What do you fear? Franklin D. Roosevelt said, "We have nothing to fear but fear itself." How true that is! Sometimes our fears are real, but often they are ideas either we put in our own heads or other people put in our heads.

1. Using a dictionary, write out the definition of *fear* that fits your situation.

   _____

   _____

   _____

   _____

2. Read the following verses about fear.

   Proverbs 29:25—What does fear do to you?

   _____

Psalm 48:6—Has fear taken hold of you?

_____

Matthew 28:1–5—Who was afraid in these verses?

_____

Luke 1:30—Who spoke "fear not" to Mary?

_____

There are many references to fear in the Bible. Some of these reflect fear directed toward God, others a reverence for God. Some show the fear of people, and some reveal terror in circumstances. God can place fear in your heart to keep you from wrong, but Satan can also place fear in your heart to cause you to doubt and not trust God.

3. Below is a list of the fears you may have had since your loved one died. Check those that have been real to you.

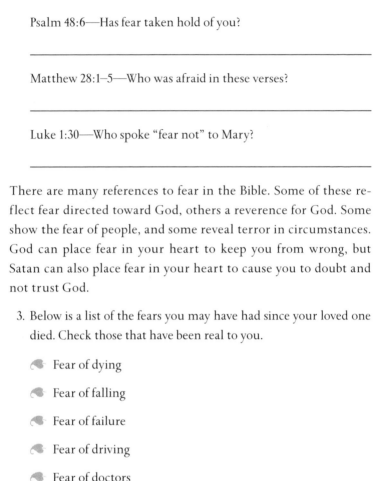

Fear of dying

Fear of falling

Fear of failure

Fear of driving

Fear of doctors

Fear of rejection

Fear of the future

Fear of being alone

Fear of failing health

Fear of others' opinions

Fear of doing new things

Fear of making decisions

- Fear of meeting new people
- Fear in the midst of confusion

All of these are real fears. Some of these I have experienced myself. Now that you have identified the fears, what do you do about them?

4. According to Isaiah 43:1–2 where is God in the midst of our fear?

_____

_____

5. When you are fearful, you will lose sleep. Fear will also reveal itself in other ways such as restlessness, forgetfulness, self-centeredness, and doubt. What promise is in Exodus 33:14 for you?

_____

_____

6. When you are alone, you often feel as though you are flying solo and your copilot is not there to encourage or support you. Read the following verses. Who is with you in your fears?

Psalm 112:7_____

_____

Proverbs 3:25–26_____

_____

Isaiah 8:12–14a_____

_____

7. Trusting God in times of fear and doubt can bring peace and comfort to your heart. Perfect love drives away your fears, and God is perfect love. Explain in your own words how these verses apply to driving away your fears.

Isaiah 12:2_____

_____

John 3:16_____

_____

Philippians 4:19_____

_____

II Timothy 1:7_____

_____

I John 4:18_____

_____

Some fear is a sin. The root of that sin is often a lack of trust—you doubt God and His ability to care for you. In Deuteronomy 28, the people sinned by doubting God. Because of this sin, God said they would have extreme doubt and fear.

8. Read Deuteronomy 28:65–67. Have you stayed awake at night counting your fears instead of your blessings?

_____

9. What can you do when you have fears and doubt the Lord by not trusting Him? Psalm 139:23–24 has some practical advice for you. What did the psalmist ask the Lord to do in verse 23?

_____

_____

_____

Have you asked the Lord to search your heart? In verse 23 David also asked the Lord to try him and know his thoughts. Why was this a necessary request? Does God already know what you are thinking? Why do you think David made this request of the Lord? You may try to deny what is really in your heart, but when you ask the Lord to try you and reveal your thoughts, then you are willing to acknowledge what needs to be confessed to Him as sin.

10. In Psalm 139:24 David asked God to show him if there was any wicked way in him. Are you ever without wickedness in your heart?

_____

Until you get to heaven, your old nature will manifest itself in many ways. Fear and doubt are real to those who are alone.

11. Grieving is not a sin, but the fear that accompanies that grief is a sin. What should you do with known sin in your life according to I John 1:9?

_____

_____

12. After you have confessed your fear as sin, do you think this sin will cause you to fear again? Who has put the spirit of fear in your life?

_____

_____

13. Doubting God shows a lack of trust. Satan put a doubt in Eve's heart by asking a question in Genesis 3:1. What was the question? Do you sometimes question what God has said or done?

_____

_____

Genesis 6–7 records the account of Noah. God told Noah to build an ark as a place of safety. Noah preached for 120 years, warning of coming judgment. But the people of that day were wicked, and only Noah and his family believed God.

14. Read Genesis 7:21. Who died because they doubted what God said?

_____

_____

God called Moses to lead the children of Israel, but Moses argued with God. He had three reasons he told God he could not lead them.

15. According to Exodus 4:1, what was the first reason he did not want to do what God asked of him?

_____

_____

16. Read Exodus 4:10. What was the second reason?

_____

_____

17. What excuses do you have when you have fear and doubts?

_____

_____

_____

_____

Look back at the list of fears mentioned in question 3. How many would you want to argue with the Lord over?

18. Are some of these real fears or imaginary fears? Can they be overcome with prayer and trust in an all-knowing God?

_____

_____

_____

I am not making light of the apprehensions that singles face, but I also have seen many widows and widowers become ineffective for the Lord because of their fears.

Will you pray Isaiah 26:3 from a sincere heart, knowing that God knows all about your fears and doubts?

Lord,

Help me to face my fears honestly, confess them as sin, and claim Your promises for protection and leading in my life. Help me to cultivate a closer walk with You so that I can have freedom from my fears and a rejoicing heart in times of doubt. I confess that You know me better than I know myself. Help me to see myself as You see me. I pray this with a heart sincere before You. Amen.

WORRY
lesson nine

*C*hapter 8 was on fear. The first cousin to fear is worry. I have seen it in the lives of so many I have counseled over the years. Is worry only in the lives of unbelievers? No, it is also part of believers' lives and a part of grief that will discourage and defeat as you try to adjust. You need to be careful that you do not confuse worry with concern. Yes, you can be concerned about your life—the present and future—but not to the point of worry.

The dictionary defines *worry* as "to feel uneasy or troubled." You may believe that you have a right to feel uneasy or troubled. You are facing the unknown and are alone going through uncharted waters.

The dictionary also lists the words *worriment*, "the act of worrying"; *worrisome*, "causing worry or anxiety"; *worry beads*, "a string of beads that one fingers to keep the hands occupied"; and *worry wart*, "those who tend to worry excessively and needlessly."

Are some people more prone to worry then others? Yes. Can those who like to finger the "worry beads" find other tools? Yes. The best tool to free you from worry is God's Word.

1. Read Hebrews 13:8. How often does Jesus change? Have you found Him faithful in the past? Will His faithfulness change with time?

_____

_____

2. Read Malachi 3:6a. God the Father and God the Son are the same. One will not change without the other. Name some things that God controls, things you see every day that do not change.

_____

_____

_____

I have not known God to sleep in and forget to cause the sun to rise, the ocean currents to stop their ebb and flow, or the stars to come out at night. The miracle of Who God is and what He does day in and day out should cause us to trust Him and not worry. That sounds easy, but you may still worry.

3. What are some things that cause worry?

_____

_____

_____

4. In II Corinthians 11:28 Paul described a concern for the churches he had served. What word does Paul use in this verse that shows he was concerned? How often did he have these concerns?

_____

_____

5. The word _worry_ originally meant "to divide, part, rip, tear apart, be anxious, distract your attention." Read Matthew 12:25a. Who

knows your thoughts? Can you make good decisions when you worry or have your mind divided? Explain.

_____

_____

Worry often will control you rather than you control worry. Matthew 6:27 shows how unproductive worry can be because we cannot change circumstances or situations by worrying.

Worry will also rob you of time, time you could spend in God's Word, time you could be reading helpful information, time you could be seeking answers and solutions, time you could be waiting on the Lord in prayer.

6. Read Matthew 6:34. Are you worrying about tomorrow, when tomorrow has not arrived? What does this verse tell you that you should do?

_____

_____

_____

Worry damages your body, distorts your vision of tomorrow, and wastes energy.

7. According to I Corinthians 6:19–20, who owns your body?

_____

You would not think of destroying a beautiful temple or church building, which has been made by man; yet you may not see how worry can destroy the body. Worry is hard on the nervous and digestive systems. It causes muscle tension, sleeplessness, headaches, distorted vision, and many other physical problems. Remember who owns your body.

8. What practical advice does I Peter 5:7 give?

_____

_____

9. Worry is something you take upon yourself. What are you to do with these worries or cares according to I Peter 5:7? Do you find this hard to do? Why or why not?

_____

_____

_____

_____

What do you think it means to "cast" our cares on the Lord? The word *cast* in this verse has the idea of giving your cares over to the Lord. When you cast your cares on the Lord, you turn them over to Him. You give Him the circumstances that have caused your cares. The circumstances surrounding a death are often varied and complex. It can take time to gain full knowledge of the death and the reality of the change. You struggle against what you do not want to accept.

In casting your cares, you may have to ask for forgiveness of someone you have wronged. An underlying cause of worry is anger. You may have issues of anger toward others. Without your realizing it, your worry can focus on decisions you made at the time your loved one was getting medical care or even decisions at the time of death. Some of the worry may come from unsettled questions you still have. Did you make the right decisions? Should you have done things differently? Should you have allowed an autopsy? Should you have gone right to the hospital? These questions can be many and varied. Re-read I Peter 5:7. Will you pray this verse back to the Lord telling Him your worries?

Matthew 6:33 tells where your focus should be. Rather than seeking a worry time, we should seek first the kingdom of God. To seek God first means that you give Him first place in your heart, thoughts, and desires. You take on His character to serve and obey Him in everything. He promised that if you seek Him first, He will give you what you need.

10. Philippians 4:6–8 are verses you can claim and pray back to the Lord with confidence that He will hear. The word *careful* in verse 6 is another word for *anxious*. What are you told to be anxious about according to this verse?

_____

Worry is like a rocking chair. It gives you something to do, but it does not get you anywhere.

Do you believe that worry is a sin? I do not know of any verse that makes that statement, but it is implied by all the verses you have looked at. Hebrews 11:6 states that it is impossible to please God without faith. Do you think the opposite of faith is worry? Let me ask you again, do you think worry is a sin?

11. To be free of worry will require some praying but also some planning—planning according to God's will. James 4:13–15 describes some people who were making plans. According to verse 13 what were their plans? What was the reply in verse 14? What was the conclusion in verse 15?

_____

_____

_____

_____

_____

You have come full circle. You are again seeking the Lord's will in decision making to free you from worry about today and tomorrow.

12. God is interested in every area of your life. What is one thing He knows about according to Matthew 10:30?

_____

13. Who has He provided for in Psalm 84:3?

_____

14. In Luke 12:27–31 God tells us He provides for the lilies in the fields and He promises to provide for us. What does He say about us at the end of verse 28?

_____

_____

It is good to plan responsibly, but it is bad to dwell on all the ways your plans can go wrong. That is worry. There is another verse in Mark 4:36 that has been a blessing to me. Our Savior had been teaching the multitude many parables. In the evening, He was having an intimate time with His disciples. He told the disciples He wanted them to get into their boat and go to the other side of the Sea of Galilee. As they were on the water, a terrible storm arose. We know the end of the story: Jesus told the sea to be calm. But what we often miss in the reading is that there were other boats on the lake. These were also being tossed about by the storm. When Jesus stilled the storm for His boat, the other boats were also saved. Jesus cared about the boat His disciples were in but also cared for the other boats. Jesus sees the storms in your life and cares about the "big boats" as well as the "little boats."

15. To whom was the Lord speaking in Luke 10:41–42? What was Martha's concern in verse 40?

_____

_____

_____

Often our concerns are in the wrong place. Rather then being involved in the worry of everyday cares, we should do what Jesus commended Mary for doing.

16. What was she doing in verse 39 that pleased the Lord?

_____

_____

_____

17. When you put first things first, your worries will fade. Read Colossians 1:18. What place does God want in your life?

_____

18. Look up the words *preeminence* and *preeminent* in a dictionary to see what they mean. Write the definition here.

_____

_____

_____

_____

If Christ has the preeminent place in your heart and mind, what will happen to your worry? If you want to be anxious about anything, be anxious about spiritual things, pleasing Him, your personal relationship to Him, and your righteousness before Him. You are not to focus on the materials things, but these may often take first place in your worry.

19. What does Colossians 3:2 say about your attachment to things here on earth?

_____

_____

_____

20. Philippians 4:19 is a verse that many have memorized but often forget when they are faced with decisions, especially when they have to make those decisions alone. What are some current needs that you want God to supply?

_____

_____

_____

_____

When you put your needs or worries on paper and begin to pray about each one, God will lift the burden and give you peace and direction, and the worry will cease. I have experienced it in my life and you can in yours. Worry is very hard to set aside. Often you cannot set it aside on your own. I have tried to give you help from the Scripture on worry. You may find it helpful to go to other Christians to get their insight into things that worry you. I believe God provides others to help you make decisions during times of trials and stress.

A final verse to claim as you seek peace in your time of worry is Exodus 33:14. In this verse, God promises His presence will be with you. Because of His presence, He has promised to give you rest.

WHISPER A PRAYER

Come, linger here with the Master,
Come with your burden and care;
Come with your sins and temptations,
Whisper, oh, whisper a prayer.
Come to your blessed Redeemer,
He is a Savior indeed;
Call and He surely will answer,
He will supply every need.
Wait at the feet of your Master,
Pray that His will may be thine;
Wait, calmly wait for His power,
Wonderful power divine.
Whisper a prayer, Whisper a prayer,
Bring Him your burden, Bring Him your care;
Wait calmly here, Jesus is near;
Whisper a prayer, Whisper a prayer.

—*B. B. McKinney*

Lord,

I have seen in Scripture that You do not change. The Lord Who has been with me in the past is the same Lord Who is with me today and will guide me tomorrow. Help me to memorize and claim the verses I have just read. If there are areas of concern where I need help, I ask that You lead me to the right people who can give me direction. Thank You for Your leading in the past and let me feel Your peace for the present. Amen.

DEPRESSION
lesson ten

When people face a major trial, they often feel depressed. Some have tried to categorize depression into one of three areas: physical, emotional, or spiritual. Godly men will not always agree on depression in a Christian's life. Is it possible for a Christian to become depressed? What is depression? Is it more than sad feelings? As we have done before, we need to go to Scripture for the answers. We need to define depression. A feeling of being sad? A time of feeling beaten down? A time when our spirits are low? We can say yes to all these questions. The King James Version does not use the word *depression*, but we see Bible characters who were in a depressed state of mind.

Before we look into Scripture, we should make a distinction between a depressive reaction to situations and clinical depression. Those who are clinically depressed need professional help, and often a good Christian counselor is able to take the depressed person to Scripture for assurance. This may require many counseling sessions over a period of time. Medication is sometimes used, but medication often treats the symptoms and not the real cause of the depression.

This chapter is not designed for those who have clinical depression, but it is for those who are facing depression because of the circumstances that have come about in their life as the result of a loved one's death. Depression can also be associated with other circumstances in our lives that cause feelings of oppression and pressure.

1. The word *temptation* in I Corinthians 10:13 is the word *trial*. What do you read about temptation or trials in I Corinthians 10:13?

_____

_____

_____

_____

Are you the only person who has faced depression or feelings of sadness following the death of a loved one? Every obituary you read about in the newspaper means pain for someone. Death is around you every day.

2. In II Samuel 22:29 what are David's words of encouragement?

_____

_____

_____

_____

3. Read Psalm 42:3. What was David's state of mind day and night?

_____

_____

_____

_____

Tears are beneficial during the time of grief. They are helpful and relieve stress, depression, and anxiety.

4. What was the question David asked himself in Psalm 42:5, 11? Have you asked yourself this same question? Have you received an answer?

_____

_____

_____

_____

_____

I have heard many people say, "You know your loved one wouldn't want you to be sad." I believe being sad is very normal, and our thinking is wrong if we feel we cannot be sad. If the tables were turned, we would expect our loved one to miss us!

Some depression can be caused by guilt. Have you felt some guilt following the death of your loved one? You can ask yourself these questions: Why did he die and not me? Did I do everything I could for him? Were there times I could have been more loving, patient, or compassionate? These questions all relate to guilt and often go through your mind after the death. I had some of these questions after the death of my first husband. I had to think through what I did, why I did what I did at the time, and if I would have done things differently if I had a choice. I realized much of my feelings of guilt were normal. Think through your guilt by asking yourself questions or talking these over with someone you feel can give you godly insight or just a listening ear.

5. David had a cure for his depression in Psalm 42:11*b*. What was his cure? Have you tried praising the Lord?

_____

_____

_____

_____

6. Read Galatians 6:2. What advice is given here that you can apply to getting help?

_____

_____

_____

7. Read I Kings 19:1–18. What was the mood of Elijah in verses 1–5? What did he do for himself in verses 6–8?

_____

_____

_____

_____

I have found that a good meal and a good night's sleep will help with depression.

8. Where was Elijah's focus according to verses 9–10?

_____

_____

_____

Depression is caused many times by being self-focused. Why me, why now, now what? Have you asked yourself these questions?

9. How did God speak to Elijah in verses 11–12?

_____

_____

God often speaks in a quiet, still voice to you, but many times you may be too busy to hear His voice.

Your depression can be caused by the criticism of other people. When people criticize you, you then question what you are doing and how you are reacting.

10. Read Psalm 37: 23. Who should be the one to direct your way?

_____

Depression can be caused by the many decisions that need to be made following the death of your loved one.

11. One of my favorite verses is Proverbs 3:5–6. What is the condition for God to lead you?

_____

_____

This verse says that you need to acknowledge the Lord in all your ways. The word _acknowledge_ means to recognize. Recognize that the Lord knows what is best for you.

12. In what areas do you need to acknowledge the Lord?

_____

_____

_____

_____

_____

13. Have you questioned the Lord about this death rather than acknowledge His will and purpose?

_____

14. Deuteronomy 33:25b is a wonderful promise for those who feel depressed. What is the promise?

_____

_____

_____

15. In Isaiah 30 Judah had turned from following the Lord and were trusting in other nations to save them. The Lord gave them some

words of advice that you can apply to yourself when you are facing depression. What words of encouragement are used in verse 15?

_____

_____

_____

_____

I see four important words in this verse that can be a cure for depression: *rest*, *quietness*, *confidence*, and *strength*. All these verses deal with our relationship to our Lord in the time of sadness and loss.

16. What are the last three words of Isaiah 30:15? Have you been resisting the Lord's help and trying to do things your way?

_____

_____

_____

17. How can you overcome being depressed and have victory over depression? Read the following verses. What is God's answer according to these verses?

II Timothy 3:16–17_____

_____

_____

II Peter 1:3_____

_____

_____

Philippians 4:9, 13_____

_____

_____

Ephesians 5:20_____

_____

_____

John 13:17_____

_____

_____

Romans 6:11_____

_____

_____

Those who are depressed often are lonely, self-focused, and with-drawn. As you age and cannot get out to be with others, you feel de-pressed; but I have also known many older people who are alone and still find something to rejoice in each day.

18. Read II Corinthians 4:16. Paul makes two statements, one about the outward man and one about the inward man. What is the out-ward man? What is the inward man?

_____

_____

_____

_____

You have very little control over the outward man besides a good diet, exercise, and sleep, but the inward man you have total control over. Is your inward man being renewed each day with the Word of God?

Hudson Taylor said, "It doesn't matter how great the pressure is. What really matters is where the pressure lives, whether it comes between me and God or whether it presses me nearer His heart."

Father,

As I study Your Word, I find assurance that You are near me all the time. Help me to feel Your presence. I acknowledge that the feelings of depression can be normal in my time of grief. I ask that You draw me close to You for assurance of Your love, Your presence, Your peace, and Your guidance. Help me to praise You for little things that happen in my life. Amen.

BITTERSWEET
lesson eleven

*S*ome chocolate is called bittersweet. How can that be? It seems as though it should be bitter or sweet but not both. In chapter 6 I mentioned that a friend suggested I write a chapter on blessings. My first thought was negative. How can there be blessings when I am hurting? The more I thought about this, the more I realized she is right. I could list the blessings I have received, but that would only be my blessings. Joy and sorrow are often close companions in the time of sorrow and trials. Where do we start when we talk about blessings? Our blessings come from God, so the place to start is with God. We will begin with a look at God's character.

1. What does Malachi 3:6 say about God?

_____

_____

_____

This is one characteristic of God that you can be thankful for. Your feelings and emotions change with each day and sometimes more often than that. Your blessings have to come from the heart. When the heart is thankful, the praise for Who God is will follow.

2. What does Psalm 92:1 say is good for us to do?

_____

_____

To give thanks and praise even in hard times? Times of death? Times of sorrow? Remember Who God is and that He does not change.

3. What does Psalm 119:68 say about God?

_____

_____

God is good and He does not change. If this is true, and it is, then what needs to change in order for you to have a spirit of praise and to rejoice in your blessings? Read Isaiah 61:3. A garment of praise! A garment is something you put on. You choose that garment. You can choose the garment of praise in times of sorrow and grief. How do you put on that garment? Let us start with your view of God.

4. What is your view of God?

_____

_____

_____

_____

5. You need to view God for Who He is. Read Isaiah 9:6. What are the names given to God in this verse? Each one of those names speaks of one characteristic of God.

_____

_____

_____

_____

6. He is given the name *Wonderful*. The word *wonderful* means excellent. Can you think of anyone more excellent than the One Who created you? List some ways that God is wonderful.

_____

_____

_____

_____

_____

_____

7. He is *Counselor*! Have you turned to the world for counsel? Can the worldly system give good counsel? Who is the best counselor? Why?

_____

_____

_____

_____

_____

8. The next name given to God is *The Mighty God*. Is anyone more powerful than God? Read Jude 24–25 for a description of the might and power of God. Because He is so mighty, what are the promises in these verses? How long will His power last?

_____

_____

_____

_____

_____

_____

9. Isaiah 9:6 also says that God is the *Everlasting Father.* How long is everlasting?

_____

Do you praise God because He is the Everlasting Father? He will always be with you.

10. The last characteristic mentioned is the one you need most. What is the last name given to God in this verse?

_____

In Job 13:15 Job makes a very bold statement. Do you think Job could make that statement unless he knew the Prince of Peace? God will give peace and blessings in the midst of your storm. You should not focus on the storm but on the One Who is in the storm with you. You cannot store up blessings and praises from the past. They need to come fresh each day.

We have seen Who God is. Now we will look at what He has done.

11. Paul gives a benediction in Ephesians 3:20–21. According to these verses who is able to do exceeding abundantly above all that you ask or think?

_____

Right now you may not be able to see how God is abundant. This may be the time to think how God has met your needs in the past. Has He been faithful and unchanging in the past?

12. What has God provided for you according to John 3:16?

_____

This is the starting place for your praise. Without eternal life you would be without hope and lost in this world and the next.

13. According to Philippians 4:19 what has God promised He will do?

_____

_____

14. What are some of the needs you have asked God to supply? Do you think He is able to meet these needs?

_____

_____

_____

_____

_____

Sometimes your needs and your wants get mixed up. Remember He has promised to meet your *needs*. Praise Him verbally when those needs are met.

You also need to thank God for what He is doing now.

15. Read Psalm 92:1–2. According to this verse, what is good? How can you show His lovingkindness? Have you tried to be a blessing to others and to tell of God's blessings to you?

_____

_____

_____

_____

_____

16. In Psalm 71:14–15 the psalmist says he will hope continually. But he also says he will do something else. What else will he do?

_____

_____

The last part of verse 15 gives you a reason to praise and bless God. What is that reason? Your days are numbered. Only God knows when you will go to meet Him and your loved ones. Until that time, each day should be a day of praise for God's blessings to you.

17. You are told in Psalm 19:14 to do something. What are you told to do? Is it always easy to have your words acceptable to God?

_____

_____

_____

You also need to thank and bless God for what He is going to do.

18. Read John 14:1–3. What has He promised those that know Him? God gives many promises in these verses. What are His first words in verse 1?

_____

_____

_____

_____

I believe God would say the same to us. Jesus knew His disciples' hearts were troubled. You may have a troubled heart, but God tells you not to have one.

19. What did Jesus promise in verses 2–3?

_____

_____

How much do we know about heaven? Not much! For some reason God chose not to reveal much about heaven. We don't know what our loved ones are doing. We don't know if they can see us. We don't know how old we'll be in heaven. We have only a glimpse, in the book of Revelation, of what heaven looks like. God is keeping much of this to Himself until He chooses to take us there.

20. God has given you a promise in Isaiah 26:3. What is that promise?

_____

_____

Will you keep your mind stayed on Jesus Christ, the eternal God?

When you have an attitude of praise and thanksgiving, you will count your blessings each day. David was able to do this through his trials and testing and even the death of his son.

GREAT IS THY FAITHFULNESS

"Great is Thy faithfulness," O God my Father,
There is no shadow of turning with Thee;
Thou changest not, Thy compassions, they fail not;
As Thou hast been Thou forever wilt be.

Summer and winter, and springtime and harvest,
Sun, moon, and stars in their courses above,
Join with all nature in manifold witness
To Thy great faithfulness, mercy and love.

Pardon for sin and a peace that endureth,
Thy own dear presence to cheer and to guide;
Strength for today and bright hope for tomorrow,
Blessings all mine, with ten thousand beside!

"Great is Thy faithfulness! Great is Thy faithfulness!"
Morning by morning new mercies I see;
All I have needed Thy hand hath provided—
"Great is Thy faithfulness," Lord, unto me!

—*Thomas O. Chisholm*

Words by Thomas O. Chisholm
© 1923. Ren. 1951 Hope Publishing Co., Carol Stream, IL 60188.
 All rights reserved. Used by permission.

Heavenly Father,

Forgive me for the times I have questioned Your leading. I ask that You give me a thankful heart and a mouth that will speak forth Your praise. Help me each day to find something to be thankful for. I am thankful for Who You are and what You will do in my life in the days ahead. Amen.

Moving On
lesson twelve

*I*saiah 30:21 tells us, "This is the way, walk ye in it, when ye turn to the right hand, and when ye turn to the left." Finishing this last chapter does not mean that your grieving can be completed in twelve chapters, but I would be failing you if we did not close with a chapter about moving on since there really is a tomorrow, a future. Yes, tomorrow will come, but you do not know what it will hold. None of us knows what tomorrow holds, any more than we knew what the tomorrow would hold twenty years ago. We are not even promised a tomorrow.

1. What does James 4:14 say about your life?

_____

Vapor—here and then gone. Does that speak so plainly about life and death? The Bible gives many references to the brevity of life. It is brief like a shadow, a flying shuttle, and a hurrying messenger. In counseling, I have often asked the question, "If you could have picked a time for the death of your loved one, when would it have been?" The answer is never! We want to put off the separation as long as possible.

If there is one area that brings on tears more then any other is the finality of the separation by death—the realization that you will never again hold your loved one, never share the pleasurable times with each other on earth, never enjoy their companionship, never sit with them in church and many other events that will enter your mind at a moment's notice. These realizations can bring on the tears and often seem more than you can bear.

But there is a tomorrow! Life will never be as it was before, but you can still have a life. Some who are reading this may have lost a child, a parent, a friend, or a close associate. Your grief is just as significant to you as those who have lost a spouse. Your life can still have direction, and the Lord can use the experience of death and grief in service for Him.

I was blessed for nineteen months with having a "tomorrow," a moving-on experience with my second husband. Now with his death, moving on is once again a reality. Life is but a vapor.

2. What are God's thoughts toward you? Read Jeremiah 19:11 and write out what this verse means to you and your situation.

_____

_____

_____

3. God desires the best for you even if you have a hard time understanding that in the midst of your grieving. In Philippians 2:13 God has a desire for you. What is that desire?

_____

_____

_____

_____

God's will should be our will, not the other way around. Have you tried to tell God what you want from Him now that you are alone?

Do you feel that His desires are your desires? How do your desires and God's desires differ? As one who is grieving, you need to reinvest your life. You need to think of moving forward and not digging in, saying or thinking that you will not move forward.

4. Read Psalm 40:8. What has to be in your life in order for you to know God's will?

_____

_____

_____

_____

_____

You will never know God's will unless you are in His Word and seeking His will through prayer and godly counsel. Reread Isaiah 30:21 to be reminded of God's promise.

For widows or widowers, moving on will involve two paths: to remain single or to remarry. There are no other choices. Is there life after death for the single person? Yes! What should be your goal as a single?

5. Read I Corinthians 7:32–33. You are reminded in these verses who you are to please as a single. Who is that?

_____

6. Think of other single people who are serving the Lord. What are some of the opportunities for serving?

_____

_____

Your service for the Lord does not have to be in full-time work or even work that other people see. Over the years, I have encouraged many singles to become involved in their community. Can this be a service to the Lord? Yes! Giving a cup of cold water in Jesus' name is a service mentioned in Mark 9:41. Acts 9:39 mentions Dorcas, who made coats for others as a service to the Lord and others.

As a single you may view the cup of your life as being half empty rather than half full. You can be a testimony to many around you by your faithfulness, your reinvestment in life, your verbal witness, and a word of encouragement to others who are hurting.

7. In Acts 1:8, Jesus told His disciples to be a witness in Jerusalem, Judea, Samaria, and the uttermost part of the earth. Those areas included their hometown, the area surrounding them, and the whole world. What areas near you needs your witness? Are you willing to use your time and abilities there for the Lord?

_____

_____

_____

_____

_____

8. Your relationship to the Lord is more important than your relationship to anyone else. What statement did Paul make in Philippians 4:11?

_____

_____

9. One of the verses I remember when I think of being a single is I Timothy 6:6. What is supposed to be your attitude toward singleness according to this verse?

_____

_____

_____

_____

As a widow, you can become very self-centered and selfish in your aloneness. Those who have adjusted and healed the best after being widowed are those who have gotten involved in helping other people. There are many opportunities.

Now let's change directions and look at moving on with dating and remarriage in mind. (Before I go any further, I want to say I hate the word *dating*. It sounds as though we are sixteen again, but I do not know of a better word to use.) You need to realize that no one can fulfill all your needs, not even another spouse. You need to have a realistic view of remarriage. We will use Scripture to back up what we are saying, but some of this comes from my heart to yours.

I believe there are several things to consider before we look at Scripture. Those who have lost a spouse because of a prolonged illness may be ready to date sooner then those who have lost a mate suddenly. You may have taken on the role of caregiver for years and now you are coming alive again.

You need to come to terms with your singleness first. This does not necessarily mean all your grieving is past. You need time to adjust to being alone. Women seem to deal with being alone better then men. As our years pile up, we really want a companion in the living room more than in the bedroom. Men often date sooner and remarry quicker. (I guess that is why God made woman for the man. He could not cope alone.) Have you noticed that women will often meet for lunch or call each other on the phone just to talk? You do not see many men gather for a meal together or call just to talk. If men gather, it usually involves work or sports, seldom just to be together. Women remarry because they want to "belong" to someone and men remarry for practical reasons—washing, cooking, and keeping house. You need to have a realistic view of your previous marriage. Was your marriage always perfect? Did you always see eye to eye on everything? A second marriage will not be perfect either. You are now bringing two people together who have established habits, many times different from the other's. (You really bring four people into the new marriage—the two who are living and the two who are deceased.)

10. When you start dating, the first area that must be settled is based on II Corinthians 6:14. What needs to be the guiding principle according to this verse?

_____

_____

_____

_____

But you say you are only dating and would not marry him or her. Every date is a potential mate. *Do not* date anyone who is not saved, growing in the Lord, and living for God. It will lead only to heartache. I have a very dear friend who was widowed for years before she remarried. Someone introduced her to a man who said he was a Christian. They dated for four months and married. Several months after the marriage, he stopped coming to church with her. Her life is one of misery and heartache. *Do not* date anyone who is unsaved.

One area that is often a major conflict in marriage is the area of finance. When you begin to talk about remarriage, finances need to be discussed.

11. What does Romans 12:17 tell you?

_____

_____

_____

If you cannot discuss finances before marriage, you will not be able to talk about them after marriage. If either of you has a history of indebtedness or bankruptcy, discuss this and seek financial advice before you say "I do." Finances, investments, views of money, and financial goals can be individual matters, but all these need to be discussed.

12. Another area that should be looked into is your past. What does II Corinthians 8:21 say? Who knows if you are being honest according to this verse?

_____

_____

_____

_____

How long have you known this person you are dating? What do you know about him? I had known my second husband for twenty-two years but only in the context of our church and the times my first husband and I had been together with him and his first wife. I felt I knew him very well, but before I dated him for very long, I went to others who had known him in different circumstances than I had. I went to some of his friends, his past fellow employees, his present employees, other church members, his family, and mine and asked for their view, not approval.

13. Would you want to be warned before you say "I do" in what could be a big mistake? Read Proverbs 27:6. What is your understanding of this verse if you are dating and considering marriage?

_____

_____

_____

_____

Keep this verse in mind if the opportunity for remarriage presents itself.

We spoke in the beginning of this chapter about coming alive again. God has made you with a desire for the opposite sex. This is normal, natural, and good. When dating again, it is natural for the flesh to come to the forefront in your relationship.

14. Psalm 119:133 gives a warning. What is this warning?

_____

_____

_____

As a Christian, you are not to have a physical union with someone else until marriage.

15. What does Hebrews 13:4 have to say about married love and sex?

_____

_____

_____

The world's view of sex is the same if you are sixteen or eighty-six. When I hear of widows and widowers beginning to date, one of the first things I say is "Stay out of bed until you marry." It does not matter if the couples are Christians or unsaved, it is still good advice. I can think of many women I counseled along these lines who went against my counsel and ended up with heartache, and they are still alone.

16. You should earnestly pray and seek God's will in any decision you make and especially when it comes to remarriage. What is the promise in Matthew 6:33?

_____

_____

Does this mean if you ask the Lord for a partner He will give you one? Not always, but if you are seeking God's will with a sincere heart, you will be satisfied with what He sends your way whether it is singleness or remarriage.

One last area that I feel needs to be covered is business and legal matters, some of which you may have handled already and some of which may still be looming out there.

17. What command is given in I Corinthians 14:40?

_____

_____

_____

_____

Paul was speaking to the church at Corinth about organization, but this verse can be applied to the business in your life. Some paperwork that may need to be looked into is your will, car title, life insurance, health insurance, hospital bills, credit cards, social security, veterans or military papers, retirement accounts, investments, checking and savings accounts, deed to your home or property, business partners, current bills, and so forth, depending on individual needs. Many of these business matters pertained to the deceased but need to be updated for the survivor. When calling about these matters, you would be wise to keep records. It is often necessary to make several phone calls to complete business matters. This process is often tiring and frustrating. Realize it will end in time. Many times, you may not think clearly during your grief or "new love," so do not sign any papers until you have a clear understanding of what is involved.

18. James 1:5 tells you where you can go for wisdom. What is your source according to this verse? How much wisdom will God give you?

_____

_____

_____

_____

Your life is changed forever by the death of your loved one. It will never be as it was before, but your life can still be useful and blessed by God. Often it is a matter of waiting on God and following His leadership. When you wait, you may not see anything happening. God will work in your life if you will allow Him to.

19. What is David's prayer in Psalm 25:5?

_____

_____

_____

Can you think of anyone better to lead your life then the One Who knows you better than you know yourself?

20. Are God's desires your desires? Psalm 37:4–5 has been a passage that has been a great encouragement to me. What are some key words in these verses that you need to claim?

_____

_____

_____

My prayer for you as you face the months and years ahead is that you allow God to use you to be a blessing to many who are beginning their journey of grief. You can be a great source of help and comfort to them.

TAKE MY LIFE AND LET IT BE

Take my life, and let it be
Consecrated, Lord, to Thee;
Take my hands, and let them move
At the impulse of Thy love,
At the impulse of Thy love.

Take my feet, and let them be
Swift and beautiful for Thee;
Take my voice, and let me sing
Always, only, for my King,
Always, only, for my King.

Take my silver and my gold,
Not a mite would I withhold;
Take my moments and my days,
Let them flow in ceaseless praise,
Let them flow in ceaseless praise.

Take my will, and make it Thine.
It shall be no longer mine;
Take my heart, it is Thine own,
It shall be Thy royal throne,
It shall be Thy royal throne.

—*Frances Havergal*

Father,
Thank You, Lord, for the blessing of marriage. Thank You for the good
times we enjoyed and for the hard times when we leaned on You. As I look
ahead, I ask that You would be my guide. If I am to remain alone, I ask
that You make me content in that. If You would lead in the direction of
remarriage, please give me wisdom and discernment. Thank You for all that
You have meant to me in my life. I ask that my life would be a blessing to
others as I let You lead me. Amen.